Spiders in your Neighborhood

A Field Guide to Your Local Spider Friends

By Patrick Stadille

REVISED AND EXPANDED

H

Heyday, Berkeley, California

Library of Congress Control Number: 2022933461

Cover Art: Patrick Stadille
Cover Design: Ashley Ingram
Interior Design and Typesetting:
        Patrick Stadille and Marlon Rigel

Published by Heyday
P.O. Box 9145, Berkeley, California 94709
(510) 549-3564
heydaybooks.com

Printed in East Peoria, Illinois
by Versa Press, Inc.

10 9 8 7 6 5 4 3 2 1

Table of Contents

This book is dedicated to my spider mentor, Darrell Ubick, and to Sierra Nevada Field Campus.

~ CONFESSION ~

I used to be terribly afraid of spiders. I would check the ceiling and under the bed each night before going to sleep. I did this for years!

After college, I became a science teacher. I started to read a little about spiders. They didn't seem so bad. My fears began to lessen. Learning the truth about things you fear often causes the fear to evaporate away.

Then one day, I heard about a 5-day class on spiders. The class was to take place at a field school in the Sierra Nevada Mountains.

"Hmmmm. Sounds interesting, but kinda spooky." Well, I took the class. It was fantastic! I was transformed! To me, spiders became fascinating, amazing, and even beautiful. They had cool parts and interesting behaviors. The class showed me all the diversity of species, colors, and shapes. Some were even kinda....um....well.... cute! "Hey! What gives? Uh...well...I....um...I guess I... love spiders now." WHAT? Wow! Me, the spider whimp, is now Captain Spider, the friend of Arachnids everywhere.

"I like you."

"THANX, buddy."

Well, since then, I have learned much about our local spider fauna. In this book, I would like to introduce you to some of your common, local, spider neighbors and their stories.

These are species or family groups that you can easily find around your house, yard, or nearby trail. Each page contains pictures, field marks, and natural history. Spider anatomy, webs, and relatives are also included.

"Hello Friend!"

"Morning Neighbor!"

Since the 1ST edition of this book, I have continued to spider snoop, meet new and old arachnids, and take pictures. Great new books on spiders have Also been published, helping me to find additional spider species that are new to me in my neighborhood.

In addition, I have added some ideas and methods to stimulate deeper spider appreciation. You'll find suggestions for field study, monitoring, sketching, and other goodies. Extra tips for catching and observing spiders are included.

Most spiders are harmless and are important to Nature as bug predators and food for other animals such as birds and lizards. Too many people fear these beneficial creatures. Spiders need human friends to educate others and protect them from being needlessly killed. Perhaps after reading and using this book, meeting your spider neighbors, taking some pictures of them, and watching some of their behaviors, you will come to love spiders too.

SAVE THE SPIDERS

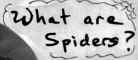

- The 49,000 species of spiders are in a vast group of creatures called Arthropods.

The Arthropod phylum consists of "jointed-foot" creatures with an exoskeleton of chitin. Insects, Crustaceans, Millipedes, and Centipedes are also Arthropods. Spiders and their relatives are a special group of Arthropods that are called...

ARACHNIDS!

"Hey Paddy! What's a critter gotta do to get in this here 'Arachnid Club'?"

- To be an Arachnid, an arthropod must have 4 pairs of legs, 2 body divisions, 0 antenna, no chewing mouth parts, and a sucking stomach. Scorpions, Ticks, Harvestmen, and others are Arachnids.

"To be, or not to be A Spider. That is the Question"

- Spiders are seperated from other Arachnids by their chelicerae with venom and their ability to "spin" silk.

- All spiders have venom which is used to kill their prey. Spiders liquify their food by the regurgitation of digestive juices in or on their dead prey. Some spiders gently suck up their meal while others mash the prey item into bits while they feed.

"Arach" is Greek for "spider."

Arachnology

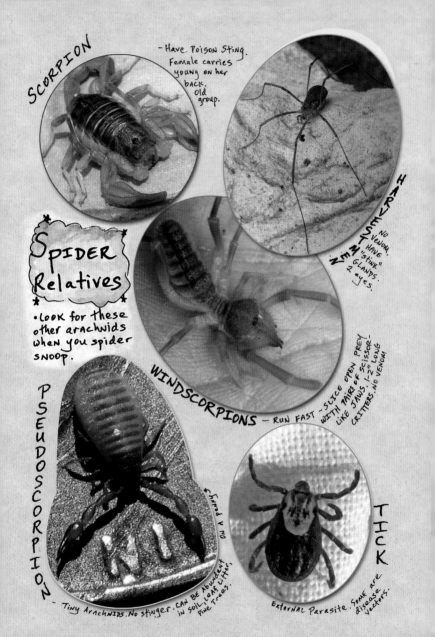

SCORPION — Have. Poison Sting. Female carries young on her back. Old group.

HARVESTMEN — No venom. Have "stink" glands. 2 eyes.

Spider Relatives

* look for these other arachnids when you spider snoop.

WINDSCORPIONS — RUN FAST — SLICE OPEN PREY WITH PAIRS OF SCISSOR-LIKE JAWS. 1–2" LONG CRITTERS. NO VENOM

PSEUDOSCORPION — Tiny Arachnids. No stinger. Can be abundant in soil, leaf litter, Pine Trees.

Shinny on a Penny

TICK — External Parasite. Some are disease vectors.

"Welcome, AMERICA, to NAME THAT SPIDER!!"

"Garden spider"
"Zig-Zag spider"
"McKinley spider"
"Zipper spider"
"Writing spider"
"Corn spider"

"Hold it players!!"

"That's a lot of different COMMON NAMES for the SAME spider."

THough these NAMES are easy to remember and proNOUNCE, you can see how they lead to confusion between different folks. IN addition, most spiders in Spiderland are unfamiliar to the public and don't even have COMMON NAMES! Same for insects.

Then how do arachnologists across the country and world communicate about a certain spider? Easy. They use—

THE Scientific NAME!

a unique, 2-word name for each kind of living thing.

The first NAME is called a genus NAME and the second is called a species NAME

A species is a population of creatures that can reproduce together. A genus is a group of closely related species.

GENUS + species = SCIENTIFIC NAME

No 2 different creatures can have the SAME scientific NAME. It can ONLY be used once. That's the rule.

Arachnology

Spider Structure and Function.

Walking Leg 1. Followed by legs 2, 3, and 4. Hunting spiders have strong and stout legs while web builders have more delicate and sensitive legs.

Palps - Used for food manipulation, courtship, sperm transfer by ♂'s.

Cephalothorax (Prosoma) The place where the appendages attach, sensory area, sucking stomach, muscles, ends of the venom glands.

Abdomen (Opisthosoma) Digestion, Heart, silk glands, respiratory areas.

Spinnerets - Tubes with many end spigots or openings where different kinds of silk are pulled out.

Chelicerae - "The spider's hands". Snip silk. Often "teeth" on inner margin for mashing prey. Most move side to side.

Eyes. Most spiders have 8 eyes, often in 2 rows of 4. Some spiders have 6 eyes. The Eye Pattern can be very useful in identifying spider families.

Palp

Fangs. Hypodermic-like structures which deliver venom to prey.

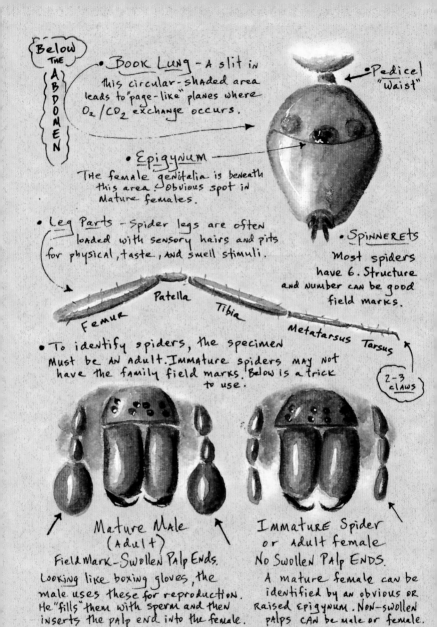

- **BOOK LUNG** – A slit in this circular-shaded area leads to "page-like" planes where O_2/CO_2 exchange occurs.

(Below the ABDOMEN)

• Pedicel "Waist"

- **Epigynum** – The female genitalia is beneath this area. Obvious spot in mature females.

- **Leg Parts** – Spider legs are often loaded with sensory hairs and pits for physical, taste, and smell stimuli.

• Spinnerets – Most spiders have 6. Structure and number can be good field marks.

Femur   Patella   Tibia   Metatarsus   Tarsus

2-3 claws

- To identify spiders, the specimen must be an adult. Immature spiders may not have the family field marks. Below is a trick to use.

Mature Male (Adult)
Field Mark - Swollen Palp Ends. Looking like boxing gloves, the male uses these for reproduction. He "fills" them with sperm and then inserts the palp end into the female.

Immature Spider or Adult Female
No Swollen Palp Ends.
A mature female can be identified by an obvious or raised epigynum. Non-swollen palps can be male or female.

The "Skinny" on Silk

• All spiders use silk. This elastic protein is used for draglines, retreats, cocoons, ballooning, and of course, prey capture webs. Silk inside the spider is a liquid, formed in silk glands. It hardens upon contact with the air as it is tugged out of the finger-like spinnerets.

Hunting Season

• Not all spiders make prey capture webs. Wolfies, jumpers, and other families hunt down their prey or ambush it. These spiders have strong legs, strong chelicerae, and usually good vision. Some are armed with spines or special hairs to aid in prey capture.

♥ Love is in the air. ♥

• Courtship is an interesting and necessary behavior in many spider families. Most spiders are cannibals, thus males trying to mate with females have to achieve mate recognition or else they become dinner. Spiders accomplish this with a variety of techniques such as web-plucking, palp-waving, dances, and even gifts of dead insects. Once accepted the male can mate with the female. Most males crawl away unharmed after mating. Even Black Widow males usually escape. Only a few species actually eat the male. Once again, another "Urban Myth", leading to fear or dislike of spiders, is dispelled.

Spider Bites

Most spiders are shy and only bite when they are squished or are perhaps guarding egg sacs. Allay those fears and worry instead about the Giants.

WEBS

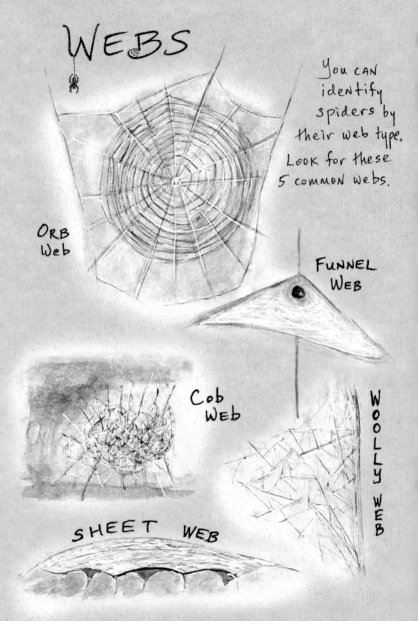

You CAN identify spiders by their web type. LOOK for these 5 common webs.

ORB Web

FUNNEL Web

Cob Web

WOOLLY WEB

SHEET WEB

Webs & Cocoons

COCOONS

— A homemade silken package, the cocoon helps to maintain a steady level of humidity, temperature, and safety for developing eggs.

↳ INSIDE a petri dish, this captive <u>Araneus</u> surprised me the next morning with her cocoon, aka the egg case.

• Above, Mama <u>Argiope's</u> abdomen was much smaller after a night's weaving. Note the "kettledrum" shape of this species' cocoon.

• I found → another in the wild. About ½" in diameter. See how it is secured to the grass with silk?

← "I say! This is a cocoon temple!" A 1" masterpiece by <u>Argiope</u> <u>aurantia</u>.

I love the color of this cocoon → from <u>Araniella</u>. Look for more cocoons in this book. They're cool!

THE MONEY SPIDER
(aka SHEETWEB WEAVERS)
FAMILY Linyphiidae

• This is a very diverse family of spiders. Many are tiny as adults. Money spiders hang upside down below the web. Look in shrubs, conifers.

• The name of "Money" Spider comes from the British lore that if a ballooning Sheet Web Spider lands on your head, you will come into money. I, of course, believe this.

CELLAR SPIDER
(aka Daddy Long-Leg Spider)
FAMILY Pholcidae

• Often confused with Harvestmen (similarly called Daddy Long-legs), the Cellar Spiders are true spiders that are common in houses and garages. Local species are likely non-native. They build a messy, cob-web like tangle. Females carry the egg sac in their chelicerae. These are harmless, despite the common myth about their poison.

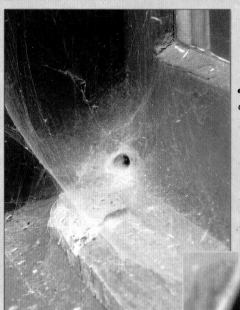

FUNNEL WEAVERS
FAMILY AGELENIDAE

- THESE spiders are COMMON AROUND SHEDS, HOUSES, AND IN BUSHES. Their web is NON-STICKY. Prey that land on the platform are QUICKLY caught by the spider who emerges from its funnel end or tubular retreat.

- These spiders have long spinnerets. The 8 eyes are in 2 rows, usually PROCURVED (Arched to the front).

- I see Agelinids often in Juniper bushes. They can be very well hidden in their retreat. Stick an umbrella under a bush, and shake the bush, and lots of spideys will land inside.

Woolly Web Spider

FAMILY Desidae

• These spiders are native to Australia. They spin a dry, blue-gray silk that is very lace-like. The silk is combed out by structures on the back legs as it is pulled out of a specialized spinneret called the cribellum.

• At night, you can sometimes see these spiders combing out their woolly silk in rapid-fire pulses. In the day Woollies are in a tubular retreat. These harmless spiders are abundant on chain-link fences, Dumpsters, buildings, etc. About ½" long.

• You might find relatives of Desids called Dictynids. They form smally lacey tangles on the tops of dry plants. They are tiny, ¼" long.

"Whoa Nellie! That's one big spider!"
This is **Callobius sp.**,
a Hacklemesh Weaver
FAMILY Amaurobiidae (Am-mor-o-bee-i-dee)

I found this female under the bark of a Eucalyptus tree. Do not fear, for she is a gentle giant. Look under forest rocks, logs, and tree bark for them.

At left is the male. My friend Cathleen found him in her house. As we will often see, this is a male spider on a lonely quest for his love

The pale spots or Vs on the dark abdomen are a good starting field mark for these large, brown-red spiders.

To confirm it's an Amaurobiidae, you need to look for a cribellum.

"Pray, wherefore art thou, fair Callobius?"

Absent in most families, this plate-like structure near the spinnerets forms woolly silk from numerous spigots.

For Amaurobiids like Callobius, it's divided into two.

Messy, hacked silk gives this family its COMMON NAME.

Woolly Web Spiders   15

THE ORB WEAVERS

FAMILY ARANEIDAE

• Many spiders that you meet in your daily spider snoops are classified into this diverse family. Most hide during the day in their "Retreat". At night, they perch in the web.

ARANEUS sp.

Araneus is a common genus of orb weaver that you might see. They form large orb webs in shrubs, trees, and outside of houses. They vary in color from orange to gray to brown. A ventral black spot and pointy shoulders are good field marks

• It's fun to feel the silken dragline on my arm as she crawls about.

• Orb weavers have lateral eyes on ridges and they are close together. Their legs can be short and spiny. Stout abdomens.

• These pictures are of females, which are especially visible in the fall because they have grown large and are ready to lay a cocoon full of eggs. They are often called Pumpkin spiders because of their shape and fall visibility. To find <u>Araneus</u> in her retreat, like you see here → , follow a side silken line to a near-by leaf or other nook and maybe you'll see a friend.

• Araneus is quite docile despite her spooky size. They are fun to watch and photograph. Good outdoor pet.

• <u>Araneus</u> is a genus, or group of closely related species. There are several species of Araneus around here. Perhaps you can identify some. Carefully notice markings, location and microhabitat, and physical features of the spider. Combine your observations with a scientific key from the internet or a good set of photos. A very honorable endeavor!

"Hmmm... what species of Araneus are thee?"

Further Travels In ARANEUS LAND

I love the size, color, and pattern variations found in this genus.

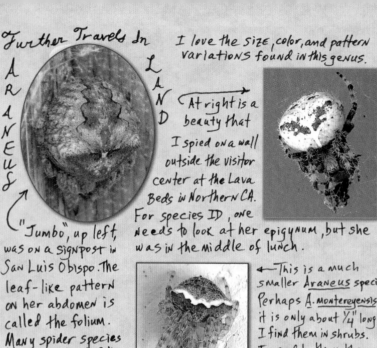

At right is a beauty that I spied on a wall outside the visitor center at the Lava Beds in Northern CA. For species ID, one needs to look at her epigynum, but she was in the middle of lunch.

"Jumbo", up left, was on a signpost in San Luis Obispo. The leaf-like pattern on her abdomen is called the folium. Many spider species have a distinct folium.

←This is a much smaller _Araneus_ species. Perhaps _A. montereyensis_, it is only about ¼" long. I find them in shrubs. I used to think these were baby _Araneus_ spiders but they are full-grown Adults!

Actual size→

Methinks her elegant cape of black and gray, speckled with crystal-like white spheres, is of royal blood indeed.

'Twas at my bank ATM where I met my true Araneus Queen! ♡

For but a few fleeting moments, her tarsus and my hand met in Love's gentle touch. Alas, "Goodbye sweet angel," said I as she crawled away to her retreat, never to see me more. Sob!

Araneus LookAlikes —

I recently got aquainted with 4 interesting Orb Weaver genera that I had previously assumed to be species of Araneus. Now, After closer inspection, I have 4 New spider friends in my Neighborhood!

(Good science habit: Observe carefully and repeat. Don't Assume!)

My first New friend is

Eustala sp.

• Snooping among some dried plants on a foggy Spring morning, I traced some lines of silk from an empty orb web. Can you

find this camouflage master on the dry flower heads? She calmly remained perched as I took close-up photos.

← As you can see, Eustala is pretty small, 1/3". I found this one by sweep netting in the same area.

• The pointy Abdomen → is a good field mark to suspect that you have found a **Eustala!**

THERE are 13 North American species of Eustala, varying in color.

I am so pleased to meet this cutie!

New friend #2 is...

Neoscona arabesca

aka the Arabesque Orb Weaver.

About ½" long, these spiders have paired, black crescents down their abdomen and lack pointy shoulders. The 4 white spots around the black ventral spot of the abdomen help to ID this spider as... Neoscona

Σ I find them in blackberry bushes at my school.

Outside my dentist's office, I found several in some nearby tules. → I guess it pays to go to the dentist.

• You may have the larger Western Spotted Orb Weaver in your neighborhood. It is in the same genus as Arabesque.

• I found this ½" long spider in a willow and shrub field near the Carmel river. I had to go on night patrol to find her in her orb web.

New friend #3 is...

Larinioides sp.

• "Larry" was easy to identify by the yellow white crescent, next to her black spot.

I found several "Larrys" during my prowl.

Final New friend #4..... **Aculepeira packardi**

These spiders are more slender and fuzzy than Araneus. I found this ¾" Orb Weaver while exploring Butterfly Valley in the Sierra Nevada. Her web was set in a boggy meadow where the insectivorous Sundew plant grows. I have also seen this uncommon spider in a grassy patch in the rugged Coast Ranges near Big Sur.

"Shall we dance amongst the orb weavers awhile longer?"

Yes indeedy, for I have many other beauties to show thee! Behold....

the **Six-Spotted Orb Weaver (Araniella displicata)**

• This is a pretty little spider that I am always pleased to find. Less than ½", Araniella is easy to identify by the 6-8 spots on her abdomen.

• My students and I find these in Oak and Buckeye trees. At right is the male.

AND NOW, MAY I INTRODUCE..

THE BIRD TURD Spider

(Cyclosa sp.) This cute orb
weaver needs no retreat!
Mottled in shades of brown
and perched in a vertical line
of debris, Cyclosa is safely
camouflaged in what does
indeed resemble, a calling
card from a feathered friend.

• This deception
is futher enhanced
by the spiders' oddly-
shaped abdomen. ↘

• These fun spiders
may vibrate their
web (like Argiopes)
to appear bigger,
when disturbed. Some
just drop to the ground.

• An examination of
the debris field under
a microscope or hand
lens will reveal B.T.'s
diet. Cool experiment.

Zygiella sp.

This non-native orb weaver spins webs around lights, eaves, and bushes.

Though in their retreat, hidden by day, you can easily I.D. Zygiella's web.

Look for an orb web with the "missing pizza slice".

If you see this, it's Ziggy.

THE Labyrinth ORB WEAVER
(<u>Metepeira</u> sp.) — These beautiful and gregarious spiders have a cryptic orb web amongst a silken tangle. Found in the tops of Coast Live Oak, Ceanothus, and Coyote Brush.

I call these "Tent Spiders" because their retreat, made of silk and debris, looks and hangs like a tent.

THE BANDED ARGIOPE
(Argiope trifasciata)

• These beautiful, half-dollar sized spiders are found in grasslands and shrubs such as Coyote Brush and Sagebrush.

• Unlike other Orb-weavers, Argiopes don't hide in a retreat. They perch in the hub, face down. Look for the Black and Yellow Argiope, (A. aurantica) a close relative nearby.

• Argiopes weave a thick, vertical strand of silk called the stabilimentum. This zig-zag pattern is found near the web center, or hub, and its function is UNKNOWN. There are many hypothesis such as prey attracting, deterring birds, etc. Perhaps you can observe and experiment and figure it out.

With her ventral (belly) surface usually facing the sun, can you see her spinnerets?

Argiopes can be abundant in some places. How many can you find in this photo?

Argiopes arrange their legs in pairs to form an X. Their leg markings help them disappear in the dry grass.

But wait! Who is this?

A STRANGER?

Nope. It's . . . the boyfriend!

The diminutive male here spins a web parallel to the female and reaches across the divide to deliver his sperm. Ah, young love. 💕

Most male spiders are smaller than females.

"But soft. What spider through yonder shrubbery breaks? It is _Argiope_. Oh it is _aurantia_."

Known by many common names, this spectacular arachnid is called the

Black and Yellow GARDEN Spider
(_Argiope aurantia_)

• Much less common in my neighborhood than _A. trifasciata_, _A. aurantia_ apparently prefers to be near wetlands and moist gardens.

• Due to its elusive presence, I am overjoyed when I find one of these in our school nature garden.

What is the black and yellow pattern all about? Are the color patterns of _aurantia_ and _trifasciata_ for the same purpose? This could be an interesting topic to study and research.

Ventral surface markings.

"Howdy Partners!"

One day a student brought me this live lovely. It is not found in my area but is a Southern Cal neighbor.

Naturally, for such a find, I gave the student an A+ for the whole year.

Silver Garden Spider
(Argiope argentata)

. "Silver" is easily recognized by the large triangular lobes edging the abdomen. I wonder why these lobes evolved? Any thoughts?

• Preferring a warmer climate, you'll find A. argentata in southern Florida and Texas.

• With 89 Argiope species in the world (5 in the US), there are many body colors and stabilimentum designs.

I've read that Silver's design is 4 small zig-zags for each web corner. I want to see that!

LONG JAWED ORB WEAVERS

Tetragnatha sp.

Humongous chelicerae and fangs explain the common name of this family. Under magnification, their awesome mouthparts may look dangerous, but they are harmless to people. I like how they perch on sticks. This spider might do this on your finger too!

• Check out this dude's choppers! Colossal!

• Notice the cheliceral teeth? The larger spines are for locking with the female's chelicerae during mating. Smart move.

FAMILY TETRAGNATHIDAE

• Unlike the vertical webs of Araneidae, these spiders build an orb web that is almost horizontal. Look for them near water, catching emerging mosquitoes.

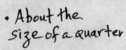

Other field marks:

• LONG legs

• About the size of a quarter

• Long, slender abdomen

• Some species live in oaks or grassy fields.

THE BLACK WIDOW

FAMILY THERIDIIDAE
(Cob Web Weavers, AKA
Comb Footed Spiders)
(_Latrodectus_ sp.)
Around 5 species in U.S.

Common in old gopher and squirrel holes, quiet corners, and hidden places, the Black Widow is a shy and NON-aggressive spider. Its bite is very

toxic, yet deaths are unusual. Immature female Black Widows often have stripes or spots. Adults are usually glossy black with the Red Hourglass on the ventral surface.

This is a mature male Black Widow. (Notice the palps?) ♂ are much smaller.

THIS elegant spider at right is an immature female Black Widow.

She will become completely black after her final molt into Adulthood.

We found this female and her cocoons under a water valve cover.

This is why you never put your hand under a board or rock unless you can see what is under it.

IN contrast to other large Cobweb Weavers, the Black Widow makes a cocoon that is pear-shaped with a parchment-like texture and color. One cocoon can contain around 300 eggs.

Why lay so many eggs?

THE BROWN WIDOW
(<u>Latrodectus geometricus</u>)

• This cosmopolitan species is a recent import into my state. I was surprised to find this female under a workbench in my backyard.

• Closely related to the Black Widow, the Brown Widow is considered less dangerous due to its timid and non-aggressive nature. While it has toxic venom, the spider injects less volume or even NONE when it bites in self defense.

COCOONS

• Brown Widows also have an hourglass mark but it's more orange than red.

• The species name fits. Notice an assortment of colorful "geometric" shapes on top of her abdomen.

• Adults vary from tan to dark brown. The spiky cocoons above helped me identify this species.

• Lives in warm climates.

FAMILY Theridiidae , GENUS <u>Steatoda</u> .

• IN the corNer of a garage or in the woodpile is a spider that looks a lot like a Black Widow, but it isn't. This chocolate brown relative is <u>Steatoda</u>, the FALse Black Widow. This NON-Native lacks the Red hourglass and is Not dangerous.

• Careful, immature female Black Widows RESEMBLE <u>Steatoda</u>.

Several years ago, I began to notice a new, large cobweb weaver in my neighborhood. Now it is the most common spider on the walls, eaves, and fences outside my house. Meet **Steatoda nobilis**.

• The same genus but a different species than the False Black Widow, Steatoda nobilis is bigger, nickel-sized, sporting a checkered pattern atop its abdomen.

• This spider is non-native and unfortunately could be invasive.

• Invasive species take over and disrupt local food webs.

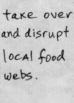

↶Here is Mr. nobilis.

⟶ Ms. nobilis, perched in her retreat. Can you see her shiny eyes?

• The Cobweb Weavers are the 3rd largest family in Spiderland. Don't let fears of Widows spook you away from an interesting group to study. For example, this <u>Enoplognatha</u> (at left) is one of many colorful Ther-i-dee-i-dees found in trees.

• Most Cobweb Weavers like <u>Parasteatoda</u> here → have a large, circular abdomen and long, spineless legs. Theridiidae are also called Comb-Footed Spiders due to the row of curved spines (setae) on the 4th leg tarsus. The spider uses this to "comb out" the silk during prey capture.

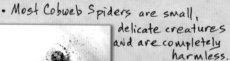

The cobweb is a messy tangle with taut, sticky triplines attached. Prey that trip these lines get flung up into the tangle.

• Most Cobweb Spiders are small, delicate creatures and are completely harmless.

• I've seen these tiny weavers, named <u>Theridion</u>, on the walls around my school. They have pretty colors and an abdominal stripe like stepping stones. Look for this common friend around the outside of your house.

THE Wolf Spider
FAMILY LYCOSIDAE

• Wolfies are hunting spiders commonly seen on the ground, in grass, amongst weeds, or on rocks along a stream. Harmless and abundant.

• Using a hand lens, Wolfies are easy to recognize. Look at their eye pattern. The posterior eye row forms a box, if you were to connect the dots. The anterior eye row is made of 4 small eyes in a line. So if you see a box of 4 large eyes its a Wolfie. No other spiders have it.

• Female Wolf Spiders are often seen carrying a large, white-ish egg sac attached to their spinnerets. Hatchlings congregate and ride on mamma's abdomen. Look closely at Wolfies with large abdomens. You may see many eyes!

Wolf Spiders   35

THE GREEN LYNX SPIDER
FAMILY — Oxyopidae

This is one of my all-time favorite spiders. Hopefully you will find one too because they are just cool. Beautiful and docile, **Peucetia** is a hunting spider in bushes and grasses.

GENUS — Peucetia

• This individual was found on a Buckwheat plant in the fall. It later made a large, spiny egg case.

• Notice the hexagonal eye pattern. This is a great field mark for this family.

• Other field marks are the spiny legs and the pointy abdomen.

• It's fun to look up the etymology (origin) of scientific names. In Greek, "oxy" means sharp and "op" means "in appearance." Now that family name makes sense to me!

• About 1" in body length, ← this spiny Green Lynx Spider can jump and move fast!

• In early October of 2020, I was elated to find this female <u>Peucetia</u> guarding a large cluster of hatchlings. A 1" diameter ball of hundreds of green legs! What a magnificent scene to behold!

• I watched and filmed Mama guarding her babies over the next 2 weeks as they gradually dispersed. She would rotate and face me when I moved to the other side of the plant. She reached the end of her life a few weeks later. I look forward to seeing her descendants in the future.

• I counted 30 abdomens in one picture. I imagine that there were many more.

• Another Lynx genus is <u>**Oxyopes**</u>. These 3/8" - 1/2" long spiders, marked in various amounts of brown, yellow, and white, are spiny like a cactus. Why have Lynx Spiders evolved this way? The spider manual says the spines "act as a basket to aid in prey capture." I want to see that!

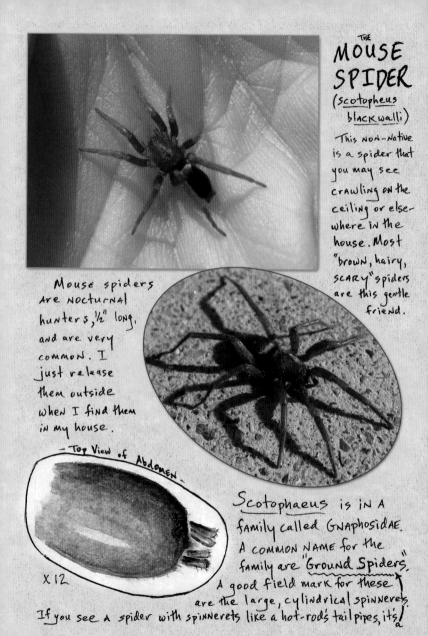

THE MOUSE SPIDER
(<u>Scotopheus</u> <u>blackwalli</u>)

This NON-Native is a spider that you may see crawling on the ceiling or else- where in the house. Most "brown, hairy, SCARY" spiders are this gentle friend.

Mouse spiders are NOCTURNAL hunters, ½" long, and are very common. I just release them outside when I find them in my house.

— Top View of Abdomen —

X 12

<u>Scotophaeus</u> is IN A family called GNAPHOSIDAE. A COMMON NAME for the family are "Ground Spiders". A good field mark for these are the large, cylindrical spinnerets. If you see a spider with spinnerets like a hot-rod's tail pipes, it's a

The GNAphosidae (Na-foe-si-dee) is a diverse spider family with 255 North American species and 2,565 worldwide. You will find these under rocks and logs or scurrying across the open ground or sidewalk. They are fast! Many are brown or black but some have cool patterns on their dorsal (backs) surface.

Say "Hello" to **Sergiolus montanus** above and to the right **Sergiolus columbianus**. ——→

I found these two goodies at my school. They are harmless hunters, about 1 cm long.

I met this 2-3mm speedster on the ground outside of our school gym. I looked at this immature spider under the microscope and I think it is a species of **Zelotes**.

• There are lots of Gnaphosids to find in your neighborhood, hot-rodding it around with their tail pipes.

Ghost Spiders

FAMILY ANYPHAENIDAE
(ANA-feen-i-dee)

• These are nocturnal hunting spiders. I often find them when sampling bushes with my sweep net. Less than 1cm long, these abundant spiders also crawl fast!

• Ghost spiders tend to be tan or light colored. Under the microscope, they are easy to ID if you look at their claw tufts.

TARSUS | METATARSUS

• Like suction cups, claw tufts are brushes or "PAWS" of packed hairs that help hunting spiders climb vertical surfaces like leaves or rocks.

THIN-haired claw tuft. Comes standard on most hunting families.

BEHOLD!

Lamelliform claw tuft, made with leaf-shaped hairs! Only on Ghosties! Costs extra for others.

Ghostie easily clings to my moving car windshield with those wide haired shoes.

Maybe Nature's invention can inspire one of your own?

Prowling Spiders
Family Miturgidae

- With their long front legs and 4 pairs of brown shoes, **Cheiracanthium** are commonly seen and are occasional house guests.

- These pale, yellowish spiders are nighttime hunters in bushes, trees, crops, and garden plants. They are near ½" in length.

- The bite is apparently painful but not dangerous.

↰ I found this one on a white plastic flag next to a bush in our school pollinator garden.

- These spiders, like many of their relatives, build a daytime silken retreat inside a folded leaf.

- They are likely the farmer's friend for they eat crop pests.

Sow Bug Spider
(Dysdera crocata)
Family Dysderidae

- A NON-Native from Europe, found under logs & rocks.

- Officially KNOWN as the "Louse Spider", I call them "Sow Bug Spiders" because they eat S.B.s, AKA the Roly Poly.

- Notice the long chelicerae and long fangs, an adaptation for their diet.

- They make a good pet for they eat well and sowbugs are plentiful.

TENGELLIDS

← These harmless spiders are often found in houses. They are nocturnal hunters and can be identified by 2 parallel rows of spines on the tibia.

CRAB SPIDERS

- THESE colorful and interesting spiders can be found blended amongst the petals, of flowers. Maybe you have seen one with a fly or Bee held in its grasp.

- THE Crab Spiders do not build prey capture webs. THEY ambush prey, relying on their flower color camouflage.

- Extra long 1st and 2nd Legs that are held away from the body and rotated back give Crab Spiders their name. They also can move side to side like a crab.

- This species is the same as Whitey on the previous page. It's called **the Goldenrod Crab Spider** (_Misumena vatia_)?

- I've read that this species can change color to match it surroundings, from white to yellow over a few days. That would be fun to observe and test.

- Here is a different species called the **Ground Crab Spider** (_Xysticus_ sp.) Like _Misumena_, this friend is in the family **THOMISIDAE.** (TOM-ISS-I-DEE)

- **Tibellus** sp. →
This crab spider is from the family **Philodromidae**, which means "love to run." Use a sweep net in meadows to find this fast spidey.

Crab Spiders

This is **Mecaphesa** sp. I found her on some wild radish at our school.

- Resembling <u>Misumena</u>, this spider is distinguished by a a spiny cephalothorax and abdomen top. Like with many spiders, her eye pattern was also useful.

<u>Mecaphesa</u> → has wider front outer eyes.

← <u>Misumena</u>'s front eyes are all equal in size.

- Spider ID and other scientific work can be challenging and requires grit! I think it's fun though, like solving a tough puzzle. <u>Mecaphesa</u> was such a puzzle for me.

Diaea livens is the name of this oak woodland beauty. Who says spiders aren't pretty?

- Yup, Crab Spiders are an interesting family to study, but this Checkered Beetle may be taking it too far.

Sandy is a
GIANT CRAB SPIDER
Her real name
is **Olios**, in
the family
SPARASSIDAE.

• About 2"
across, she has
a flat body. A
useful adaptation
for cramped
quarters.

• A student
found Sandy in
his dad's car and
let me adopt her.

SANDY'S
SCRAPBOOK

• Sandy likes to
hunt at night
and hang out on
walls.

• She normally
lives in dry
areas of the
Southwest US.

• Notice how her
tarsi lay flat
like feet?

• Claw tufts
and a brush of
hairs below the
tarsi, called the
scopula, help her
wall climb.

A cork wall and some
ROCK slabs in a terrarium made a nice home for my pet.

She starts to
weave a silken
retreat for what
would be . . . →

* *Sandy's Big* *
Adventure !!

Sandy hides inside her
parchment-like retreat.
Is she molting? I can't see
her. 2 months pass. Is she
still alive? I hear a scream! I see Sandy
escaped and out on my couch. I am joyful
but my wife is not. Oops. Back at home, the
mystery is solved when 17 babies emerge!
'Twas not a retreat, but a cocoon!

Family Salticidae

• Jumping Spiders are the "butterflies of the Spider world", for they are unmatched in their beauty and diversity of colors. They're cool.

• These jumpers are members of a genus called <u>Phidippus</u>. They are large (about ½" long) and tend to have iridescent chelicerae and reddish abdomens.

← This one gave me a little nip. Youch! No hard feelings.

• Jumpers are easy to identify. They always wear sunglasses! Look at those huge, anterior median eyes. Nice shades, MAN

• Jumpers need those big eyes for their daytime hunting and stalking of insect prey. They have the best vision in "spider-land," excellent at judging depth and seeing color.

Like most spiders, there is sexual dimorphism, with the males different in color than females. Some species are "Ant Mimics". Their 2 body divisions are elongate and they often walk with the front legs raised up like antenna.

• I photographed these 2 cuties in my backyard. Jumpers make fun pets, especially when you feed them!

Jumping Spiders

"Greetings! Besides our personality and good looks, we jumpers lead the Spider order in diversity. 5,300 world species, with 315 of them in North America, should keep you busy with camera and field guide."

♥ Phidippus

You can find jumpers in most any land habitat. The beach, garden, forest, grassland, and even the desert have Salticids.

While hiking in the glacial country of the High Sierra, I met this cutie. I was amazed to find a jumper in such a barren landscape.

"Most of us jumpers are small, about ¼" long."

FYI, Jumbo

← I found this masked marvel while sweeping through grasses and shrubs with my bug net.

↑ This is **Metaphidippus.** → Sounds like a philosopher. What do you think those markings are for? I'll give you a hint, it's the males that have all of the bling.

Jumping Spiders   49

This stripey jumper caught my eye while I was in the Pacific Northwest at a ukulele festival.

- Jumpers can be very challenging to ID to species. Stripey is in the genus **Salticus.**

(I let him go and returned to uke class.)

- I found this little jumper → in the forest at Sierra Nevada Field Campus.

Close up, he seemed rather plain, when . . .

SHAZAM!!

"Yo! Let's get this party started!"

Ladies and gents, introducing **Habronattus,** the Disco King of Spiderland! Look at those red pompom palps and that sparkly blue dance shirt! What female could resist this fashion plate?

Jumpers. They're grrrEAT!

Sometimes you meet some strange characters at the local diner or flea market. It's the same way in Spiderland. This section is devoted to spiders who have evolved some strange behaviors or looks. I affectionately classify these "free spirits" as ....

THE WEIRD SPIDERS

• Our first stop is a seldom seen, oddly shaped spider. May I present:

Rhomphaea fictilium. →

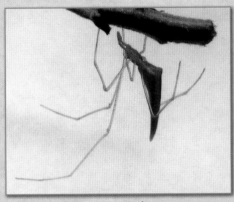

• This 1cm long Cobweb Weaver was found by sweeping some bushes at our school.

• Look at that long abdomen! Crazy, man! The female's is even longer and she can bend and wiggle it. Why? It is still unknown to science.

• Rhomphaea invades other spiders' webs and often eats the host. Yep, weird.

• A cool original like Rhomphaea needs a cool common name. You can propose one to the American Arachnological Society. Any ideas?

Weird Spider #2. → *Argyrodes* sp.
AKA the DEWDROP SPIDER

- Closely related to <u>Rhomphaea</u>, this tiny spider is one that I found near the edge of an Argiope's orb web.
- The proportion and triangular shape of the abdomen is interesting and strange.

- Sometimes silver, they can resemble a drop of MORNING dew, hence the name.

But wait! There's MORE ↓

- <u>Argyrodes</u> has an unusual behavior. It's A KLEPTOPARASITE! It sneaks into another spider's web and eats smaller caught bugs or remains while the host spider is busy eating other bugs or is unaware.

Hmm...very clever! Sounds like my teacher buddies at a staff party.

"Psst—Hey you! Yeah you. C'mere. You want weird? I gotcha. How about a species of Jumping Spider that has evolved into the shape of an ant? Nah, I'm not kiddin' ya, My name is **Synageles**, FAMILY SALTICIDAE. Ant Mimic Jumping Spider at your service!"

• A very curious and clever 8th grader named Chloe found this tiny spider on a Black Sage bush. I just thought it was an ant but Chloe used a microscope and declared, "It's a Jumper. I think it's an ant mimic." I peeked. "By Jove, I think she's got it." I am so proud of that kid. Good arachnology!

• Close up, you can see how the abdomen is long and skinny, with 2 white markings to suggest a segmented abdomen.

• Synageles also wave their 2nd pair of legs over their prosoma to mimic ant antennae.

Pretty sneaky, huh?

"Ahem! There are other weird ant mimic spiders besides that silly Jumper!"

Regards,
Castianeira thalia

Time Out! What exactly is a mimic?

- A mimic is a creature that gains protection from predators by re-sembling a dangerous model.

- True! These 2 spiders are in the

FAMILY CORINNIDAE,

THE

ANT MIMIC SPIDERS

C. thalia above is about ¼" long and ultra speedy.

"Yep! You see, predators leave us alone because they think we're stinging ants, when actually, we are just harmless spiders. Heh, heh shhh...."

— Castianeira occidens

C. occidens, ½" long, may mimic a power-ful stinging wasp called a Mutillid Wasp, AKA Velvet Ant!

- If you are ever in a sketchy situation, mimic a dangerous model like our spider pals have taught us. I mimic a poisonous slug to dissuade those who might wake me when I nap.

WEIRD SPIDER #5.
THE Flat-Mesh Weaver
FAMILY Oecobiidae

Let me introduce you to a very small spider friend that will always be your companion if you are lonely in the city. Look on outside walls, checking any small web or or spot... THERE'S ONE! →

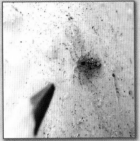

Full grown, "Tiny" is 2-3mm long.

They make a flat, circular, or star-shaped web.

← Centered on another web layer, below the dusty top web, lies Tiny Tim. See him?

His real name is ↗
Oecobius sp.

Weird Field Marks:

Pointy tip ↓ on a round cara- pace.

- Pronounced EE-co-bee-us, this odd spider is a non-native that can be found all over the world.

- I find clusters of these on the outer walls of our school.

- They capture ant prey by "corralling" it with bands of silk released while quickly running around it. Weird!

- Under a microscope, Oecobius has interesting field marks.

2 large "combs" of many "setae" (stiff hairs) near its spinnerets. This device helps comb out the silk during "round up."

- Such a peculiar and abundant spider with interesting behaviors. Oecobius. I like them.

Well our last stop in the world of **WEIRD** spiders is a cryptic critter with a new take on the traditional orb web design. It is called **Hyptiotes**, the **Triangle Spider!**

FAMILY Uloboridae

• Named for the triangular —

shaped web that it makes for prey capture.

• Hyptiotes (Hip-tee-oh-tees) uses its front legs to keep a connecting line to the triangle web extra taut. When a bug hits the sticky silk, the spider releases the tension and further ensnares the prey.

• Less than ½" long, the Triangle Spider has a bumpy abdomen and a back-row of eyes strongly curved backwards

— See Hyptiotes at my fingertip?

• Triangle Spiders are unique, for they lack venom! They wrap up their prey tight and liquify their meal by expelling digestive juices on it. Soup's on!

Around 90% of all spider families are classified into a group called Araneo-morphs. Like Jumpers, these spiders share features such as side-to-side moving chelicerae, 1 pair of book lungs, and a type of sticky silk that can act as a glue to surfaces or other silk.

"Hi! I'm an Araneomorph."
♥, Jumpy

MYGALOMORPHS

↖ This is a collection of spider families that are designed a bit differently than Araneo-morphs. Tarantulas and Trap-doors are good examples.

THE Mygalomorph design:

Chelicerae that point forward and move up and down

Usually large and hairy

2 pairs of book lungs

Eyes clustered on a central mound.

Long life span (some up to 25 years)

Non sticky silk

None of North America's Mygalomorphs are dangerous. Let's meet some!

Live in a burrow. Ambush Predators.

California Smooth Tarantula

Family Nemesiidae, (<u>Calisoga</u> sp.)

These 1.5-2" long spiders are often mistaken as baby tarantulas. They actually are full grown spiders of a different family.

Amorous males are sometimes seen in or near houses as they search for females, who live in burrows. These spiders can be fiesty when disturbed. They raise their front legs and show off their chelicerae.

CALIFORNIA TARANTULA

(<u>Aphonopelma</u> sp.)

Family Theraphosidae

Tarantulas are gentle spiders that are fun to watch and hold. The very soft touch of their legs on your hand will charm you. Males in search of females in their burrows are a frequent sight in the fall. Sometimes tarantulas flick barbed hairs off of their abdomen for defense.

Mygalomorphs

CORK-lid Trapdoor Spider

FAMILY Ctenizidae — With a PhD from the college of mining and engineering at Arachnid State, these robust spiders build silk-lined burrows featuring a thick, hinged, cork-like lid.

• Only outside of the burrow for these photos, this pet trapdoor crawled back inside where they normally spend all of their lives. Males will leave their burrow to find a mate.

• The lid is built with different layers of silk and moist soil. Very cool.

• This amazing artist uses tools such as lateral spines on its front legs and a row of spines near its fangs to build its hideaway.

The cryptic cover fits snug and can be held closed by spidey gripping it with its fangs.

Mygalomorphs

The Folding-door Spider
FAMILY Antrodiaetidae
(<u>Antrodiaetus</u> sp.)

← This Mygalomorph has a flexible, silk-lined burrow rim that can be pinched closed during the day and remain open during dinner time.

Because they blend in superbly with the surrounding grounds, I can't find the closed burrows during the day after seeing the open traps by flashlight the night before.

• The 3 tergites, dark and hardened plates on the abdomen, are a useful field mark.

• This mellow male was found in a tent by 2 boys at the Lava Beds. After a photo shoot and some show and tell to our group, we let this male return to his job of finding a female.

← Notice this cluster of thick spines below the tibia? Also a good field mark, these are used by the male to restrain the female during mating.

Hmmm... Mysterious holes!

• Do you see a pattern going on here?

• This one shows a silk-lined collar. It feels kinda flexible. The opening. Diameter estimate?

• This one is built up. What does it remind you of?

• How could you figure out how deep this hole is?

↑ • What does the tan debris indicate? See anything else?

↓ • Notice the radiating sticks? How might you test their function?

Compare the 2 holes

vs.

• Observations, questions, hypotheses?

Mygalomorphs

"Welcome to my castle, friend!"

"So glad that you dropped in!"

This is the occupant from one of those "mysterious holes."

Aptly NAMED after the small tower built atop of her burrow,

The **CALIFORNIA** Turret Spider
(<u>Antrodiaetus riversi</u>)

FAMILY
ANTRODIAETIDAE

With carefully arranged, radiating signal sticks CONNECTED to her silk-lined burrow, the Turret Spider waits inside, below the rim, for her insect prey. A beetle or Harvester ANT bumps a stick and out pounces <u>Antrodiaetus</u>! IN a flash, the spider grabs, bites, and carries her prey to the dark depths of her 1-foot burrow, where it is "DINNER for one."

These 1" long spiders use their fangs and "rake-like" ridge on their chelicerae to dig their burrow.

Offspring often burrow Nearby creating a "colony" of turrets, big and small, depending on their age.

Mygalomorphs

Spider Science

Now that you know a bit about spiders and who may be crawling around, perhaps you would like to explore deeper into the spider universe. It can be challenging, but fun!

YOU

A R A C H N O L O G I S T

N A T U R A L I S T

Many aspects of various spiders' lives are still unknown to science.

A curious and clever person like you can contribute to the body of spider knowledge.

A person who scientifically studies spiders and their relatives.

A person who observes and records the stories of Nature and her creatures.

By using:

- Repeated observations and tests
- Discussions of ideas with others
- Research from other scientists found online or in books.

Such as:

- Prey capture and diet
- Enemies and defense
- Behaviors
- Population and geographical range

* THIS SECTION OF THE BOOK WILL GIVE YOU SOME IDEAS * AND TIPS FOR DEEPER, SCIENTIFIC SPIDER STUDY.

Spider Science I
THE Outdoor Pet Spider!

1. FIND a web spider that lives in your yard or on your porch and is easy to watch. It could be a nighttime pet. (NO BLACK WIDOWS)
2. Don't capture or disturb it. This is your wild pet. Let it behave naturally.
3. Give your pet a name.

Let the science begin!

With an open and curious mind, study your pet and really get to know it. Ask questions, make hypotheses, and make comparisons. Discover amazing things just by quietly observing and thinking without distractions.

Here are some things to observe.

• What are all of its colors and how are they arranged?

• Study its legs. Are they all the same? Any spines or combs?

• Try sketching it.

• Collect numbers: Length, width, web diameter, # of radial lines, or # of spiral rows.

• What do its various shapes, colors, textures, and adaptations remind you of?

Write down your observations. See the pages on field notes, sketching, and nature journaling for ways to record your data. You may emerge with more questions than answers. That's great! That's science! Good Work!

~ Experiment Time ~

How does your pet spider respond to certain stimuli?
Let's find out, shall we?

Below are some questions to investigate. Maybe you'll think of some too. Take care not to hurt your spider or yourself.

LIGHT

How does spidey respond to light?
What about red light?
Direct light vs. side light?

SOUND

Do spiders react to music?
Does music type affect reactions?
What about your voice and different pitches?

VIBRATIONS

Test how your spider responds to vibrations. by touching the web with a "struck" tuning fork or a hand-vibrated twig.

SMELLS

Do spiders react to strong scents? Wave or waft some perfume, rubbing alcohol, vinegar, or nail polish towards spidey. Well? Any patterns?

FEEDING

Does your spider eat all insects or only certain kinds? Toss some in the web and see. Compare times of the spider's attack/wrap sequence with prey type. Where in the web does the spider eat the prey? Fun!

TIME AND SEASONS

What time of night does your spider appear in the web? When on the calendar do you first and last see it? Document size changes vs. time. When during the night does the spider repair her web? How does your spider respond to cold, heat, rain, or wind during various seasons?

Spider science   65

Spider Science II - The Captured Spider Study!

A good arachnologist or naturalist also enjoys a detailed study of captive spiders. Spiders that are safely and humanely cared for in vials or terrariums will help you to study them up close and without them getting away.

My study. ⬎
← Brief study subject.

• You'll need a good place to do this careful study. Convert your bedroom or closet to a spider laboratory.
(I might add a secret passage too.)

• A magnifier, phone camera, and nature journal will help you see cool details that you might miss outside.

• I caught this Agelenid under a rock in my yard. I put it under a microscope. Boss!

✴ Possible topics for your laboratory ✴

CHOW TIME

Watching feeding is amazing. Does your spider mash up its prey or gently feed? How does it respond to different prey species?

Maternity Ward

A captive female may spin a cocoon. How long before babies emerge? How many emerge? Will they eat tiny bugs? Each other?

INSPECTION

A detailed, close-up study of eye patterns, spinnerets, fangs, legs, claws, etc., is fascinating. Buy a close up lens for your phone camera.

Set spidey free when you are done. It would mean a lot to the spider.

Spider Science III — Who Lives Here?

How many species or families of spiders live in your yard or neighborhood? How many orb webs do you see when you walk around the park or grassland? How do these numbers change over the season or years?

- Making lists and recording data over an extended period of time can teach you about spider life cycles. The data could also be useful for detecting an environmental change.

- Naturalists and professional scientists do this with all sorts of organisms such as plants, birds, and butterflies. Spiders too!

- It would take too long to search for spiders under every leaf or rock.
- Instead, scientists SAMPLE. They survey part of the study site to get a good idea about the whole place.

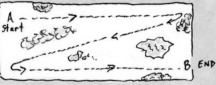

BACK YARD TRANSECT

A Start

B. END

A great sampling tool is the...

TRANSECT!

- A transect is a walking survey. Observing on a set and repeated path from A to B, you record who and how many you see.

House Exterior Transect

- It's okay if you can't identify the species or family. Give it a name that helps you remember it like Yellow Fellow or Hairy Dude. I find spiders that I can't ID all the time but I still study them.

Along your transect (walking survey) you may sample for one species, family, or all spiders. To the left are some search methods that you may use on your walk. Your goals will determine your methods. A simple walk or a thorough inspection both have their place.

• An easy way to record useful data is called a **Tally Chart.** This is a 2-column table where you make a mark for every spider that you see. For repeated study, get a small journal and make a new Tally Chart for each time you walk your transect. The more times that you repeat your survey, the more accuracy increases. Always record the date, location, and weather.

My yard, Spider City, CA
5-24-21, Sunny, 12:30 pm

Spider	# Seen
Big Jumper	I
Wolfie	ﬀﬀ I
Bird Turd	ﬀﬀ ﬀﬀ II
Money sp.	ﬀﬀ I
Little Brown	I
UNKNOWN Orb Weaver	III
Crab	II

• Enter all your data into a computer spreadsheet for easier analysis, and convert it to a graph.

• What do you learn from your data? What new questions arise?

"Question"

Spider Science IV - "Species Expert"

Do you have a favorite local spider species? Are there plenty of them around to observe? If so, you may want to become a local expert on them.

• One of my favorite spiders is ← <u>Argiope trifasciata</u>. I wanted to learn more about them. Luckily, at my school, I could observe many individuals, compile lots of data, and then look for patterns in behavior, looks, or ecology. I'm not expert yet but I've learned a lot and have had fun being an arachnologist. <u>You</u> can too!

← This is my study site. Yours may be your yard, a park, a neighborhood garden, or an open space.

• To the right is an overhead photo of my site from Google Earth. →

• First, I wanted to determine the population size and distribution of <u>A. trifasciata</u> within this grassland habitat. Students helped me find spiders which I then recorded with dots on the map.

• You could draw a map of your spider site and/or use an overhead photo like I did. I make a new map every year for this species and then compare the maps. What might I learn?

• My students ⟶ liked being arachnologists and helping me in my study. Maybe you have some buddies to help you?

• An expert wants to learn other parts of a spider's story

• Below are some other questions we asked and data that we collected on *A. trifasciata.*

Web	Orientation
Direction	# of Spiders
N	0
NE	0
E	0
SE	4
S	7
SW	4
W	0
NW	0

What directions do they face? Are they found in particular plants?

Oct. 2015	Argiope	Webs
Plant Species	Below Trail	Above Trail
Dry Grass	22	25
Sagebrush	17	2
Coyote Brush	1	11

Do they all make a stabilimentum?

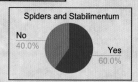

Spiders and Stabilimentum
No 40.0%
Yes 60.0%

• What details would you like to learn about your spider species?

• Along your path for more spider knowledge, use your creativity to design ways to discover more about your species. Combined with good science, observing, and thinking skills, you will become expert!

FIELD NOTES

A good naturalist or scientist records their observations, for they may be of value someday. Unwritten spider data fades from the memory like a ballooning spider lost in the WIND. Luckily your solution is to take

FIELD NOTES!

Below is the recipe for field notes developed in the early 1900s by a field scientist named Joseph Grinnell. Use this format for a day's summary or a focused study on 1 species.

Title

Name and Year

Location, from specific spot to state

Month and day

Weather conditions

Write what you see

Focus on recording detailed facts, for these are scientific notes.

You may include:
• Lists of species with numbers seen
• A map or diagram
• Purpose of the trip

Numbers and descriptive words are your tools.

Studella, P
2014

Observations on A. trifasciata

Grassland, MEarth, CMS, Carmel, CA
— Clear, sunny, ≈ 70°F

Oct 28. I observed Argiope trifasciata in a Sagebrush bush in the northern section of the habitat grassland. I watched the palps spinning and rotating the insect prey item. The web has a vertical diameter of 30 cm. The distance from the hub to the top of the web is greater than the hub to the bottom.

My students and I did some feeding experiments on some different, nearby individuals. 1 Argiope wrapped a Honey Fly and retreated to its hub in 15 seconds. A smaller Argiope wrapped a yellow Jacket in 1-2 minutes. It paused to groom its front legs after 20-30 seconds and then poured again, perhaps after biting, at 68 seconds. I noticed a 2-3 mm wide, band of silk comes out of the expanded, brown spinnerets. I wonder if prey size and type affect wrap time.

Write well and proofread your work.

Another way to record your arachnid observations is with

Nature Journaling

This is a free-form, creative page of words, sketches, numbers, and diagrams that you record from your observations and time with Nature.

Here is a recent Nature Journal page about spiders in my yard.

• It's easy to do. Pick any spot on the page and start sketching or writing.

• Sometimes I work on just one detailed sketch. Don't worry about perfection. Just Journal

• Relax and have fun. Be the spider.

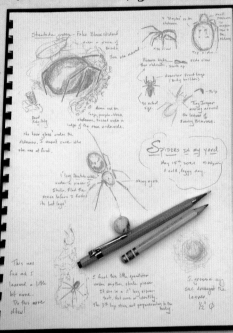

• At other times, I'll make many quick sketches, notes, and diagrams of spidey stuff that that I notice.

• All you need is a pencil, paper, and some curiosity.

Recording wildlife observations in journals with many detailed illustrations and writing makes us masters of observing. Nature journaling on spiders will help you notice and remember all sorts of cool spider things. So much that one day, you may become a Spider Master.

SKETCHING SPIDERS
in 5 steps!

↑ My photo of Zelotes.

(1) <u>Observe</u> – Take time to study your subject. Draw a faint posture line with beginning and end points.

O △
O □
↑ sketch BFFs.

Ovals helped me start.

(2) <u>Shapes</u> – Find and use simple shapes to draw the basic form of spidey's abdomen and prosoma. Draw these lightly. You'll draw over them.

(3) <u>Sculpt</u>

Turn those simple shapes into accurate body divisions. Slow down the pencil.

Looks More spidery.

Look for angles to get the shape correct. Add faint lines where each leg starts and ends.

(4) <u>Proportions</u> – Check and fix any parts that aren't the correct SIZE in relation to others. Is the abdomen too big? Are the legs too SKINNY? "THOU MUST FIX THESE!"

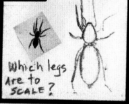

Which legs Are to SCALE?

Values
L
M
D

(5) and last.. <u>Details</u>

Look for little things to make it real: Hairs, spines, leg joints. Bring your sketch into life by finding the lighter spots and shading away. Try to have light, medium, and dark values in your sketch.

A fine sketch in 5 steps. Well done!

Left hand Light

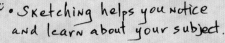

SKETCH TIPS!

- Sketching helps you notice and learn about your subject. It will make you a better observer, the most important skill of an arachnologist.

- Early on, sketch light and loose. Be "gentle with the pencil." No heavy lines. Just ballpark shape.

- Notice how I started with tri-angles and squares? Ovals helped me with the leg shapes and positions. Still gentle, loose, re-laxed and having fun.

- Step back...take a look --oops. I made his head too big. Well, I'll just draw the correct shape over those light lines. No problema.

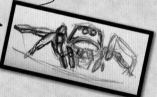

- Proportioned, I start to add details and interesting hairs, shadows, and colors are revealed to my eye by sketching. I discover so much.

Everybody can learn to sketch, so jump in.

Draw often, inside, outside, in the car, in class, everywhere!

Quick sketch master-piece, stick figure, doodle, cave painting— just draw!

Pencil, pen, crayon, chalk. Draw with friends, while you talk!

Helping Our
Spider Friends

Spider?! Attack!

So many people are needlessly afraid of spiders that a wayward jumper, a bathtub Tengellid, or an inconvenient Araneus in its web is quickly destroyed by shoe or spray.

Cease Hostilities!

You can help both spiders and fearful folks by using your spider knowledge super-powers. Explain to others about spiders' importance as insect predators and their generally harmless nature. Dispel myths.

Spiders could benefit from an ambassador such as you!

UNFORTUNATELY, THOUGH, FAR GREATER THREATS TO SPIDERS AND ALL WILDLIFE AND ECOSYSTEMS ARE CAUSING TERRIBLE POPULATION DECLINES. THE MAIN ONES ARE:

Habitat Destruction

Pesticides and Herbicides

Climate Change

Let's help stop this! Spiders and Nature are depending on us. Join me and millions of other folks who care about the environment. There are so many ways to become part of the solution. Here are a few: →

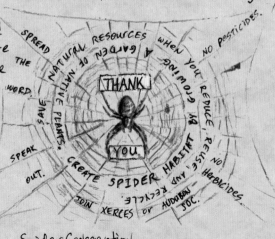

SPREAD THE WORD. SAVE NATURAL RESOURCES WHEN YOU REDUCE, REUSE AND RECYCLE. NO PESTICIDES. NO HERBICIDES. JOIN XERCES OR AUDUBON SOC. CREATE SPIDER HABITAT BY GROWING A GARDEN OF NATIVE PLANTS. SPEAK OUT.

THANK YOU.

How to Find Spiders

Now that you know some of the spider friends that could be in your neighborhood, what are you waiting for? Go find them!

- Draw, photograph, observe, experiment! They are everywhere!

- Carefully look for spiders or silk on plants, fences, under rocks and logs, and the outside of your house.

- Remember, "Where there's silk, there's spider." Usually.

- Use a flashlight to hunt by night like Dracula. Your spider friends, "the children of the night", will be visible in their webs!

Be Black Widow Safe! No hands in unseen places like under a rock or board. Use a stick to peek. Thanx!

- Beat and shake trees and bushes over a sheet, umbrella, or net. You'll find lots of spiders! Sweep grasses too.

! → Check yourself for ticks after bushwhacking.

Catch Ground Spiders by setting up Pitfall Traps!

"Spiders fall in, but don't crawl out."

GEAR

CUPS → WOOD, metal, or tile covers.

Directions:

1. Dig a hole deep and snug so that the cup rim is level with the surface.

SIDE VIEW

2. Put 4 stones on the surface corners. Place lid on stones to allow for "crawl and fall" space. (Keeps birds and rain out.)

PIT

TOP VIEW

3. Check trap daily.
4. Set up multiple traps.
5. Dismantle when done.

Lid
Stone
"No!"

Side View

Bagging Your Catch –

- Plastic VIALS with SNAP CAPS COME IN various sizes AND are perfect for capturing and safely housing spiders. I always have one in my BACKPACK, car, and POCKET. Don't leave home without one!

- ONCE in a vial, your spider needs close-up examination. I use a 5x jeweler's loupe. Through it, I am transported to a fascinating new world of eyes, fangs, and color. Mine hangs from a lanyard around my neck for easy inspection of each spider I find.

I buy my loupes at the-private-eye.com

- Tiny and fast spiders are hard to catch. The smart spider snooper often carries a pooter, aka aspirator. Mouth suction on one end efficiently vacuums speedy spider into the attached vial. A tiny screen prevents consumption by the arachnologist. Accidental spider ingestion occurs during suction on the wrong end or a mechanical breakdown.

※ SPIDERS MAKE GREAT Coffee table pets!

- They are interesting and free.

Try a Jumper

CAP WITH air holes

- They won't yip, yap, bark, or stink.
- You can take them on trips.
- Just don't let them dry out.
- Invite your friends over at feeding time and teach them how spiders are cool. Happy Spidering! Pat

Moist wad of tissue

Thanks to these References

Biology of Spiders by Rainer F. Foelix

Bugguide.net

Common Names of Arachnids by R.G. Breene, American Arachnological Society

Common Orb Weavers of the San Francisco Bay Area by Jack B. Fraser

Common Spiders of North America by Richard A. Bradley

Field Guide to Insects and Spiders of North America by Arthur V. Evans

Field Guide to the Spiders of California and the Pacific States by R. J. Adams

Orange County Spiders by Dr. Lenny Vincent, spideridguide.orangecounty.com

Sierran Spiders and their Allies class notes, Sierra Nevada Field Campus, Darrell Ubick

Spiders and their Kin by Herbert W. Levi

Spiders of North America by D. Ubick, Paquin, Cushing, and Roth

Spiders on the Web (and other Arachnids) of Orange County, CA by Peter Bryant, nathistoc.bio.uci.edu/spiders/index.htm

Widow Spiders and Their Relatives, UCIPM, R.S. Vetter